VOCAL

ROCK BAND 2

ISBN 978-1-4234-8081-5

HAL•LEONARD®
CORPORATION
7777 W. BLUEMOUND RD. P.O. BOX 13819 MILWAUKEE, WI 53213

T0056331

Visit Hal Leonard Online at
www.halleonard.com

CONTENTS

Alive

Music by Stone Gossard
Lyric by Eddie Vedder

Moderately slow Rock

"Son," _____ she said, "Have I got a lit-tle sto-ry for you. _
While she walks slow-ly a-cross a young man's _ room,

What you thought _ was your dad-dy was noth-in' _ but a... While _ you were sit-ting
she said, _ "I'm read - y for you." _ I _____ can't re-mem-ber

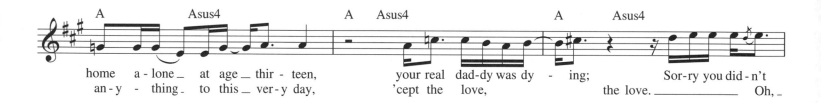

home a - lone _ at age _ thir - teen, your real dad-dy was dy - ing; Sor-ry you did-n't
an-y - thing _ to this _ ve-ry day, 'cept the love, the love. _____ Oh, _

see him. _ But I'm _ glad _____ we talked." Oh, _____
_ you know where, now I _____ can see. _____ I just _

(1.,3.) I'm _____ oh, _____ I'm still a - live. _ Aay, _____ I'm, _____ oh,
(2.) stare, _____ I, _____ I'm still a - live. _ Aay, _____ I'm, _____ oh,

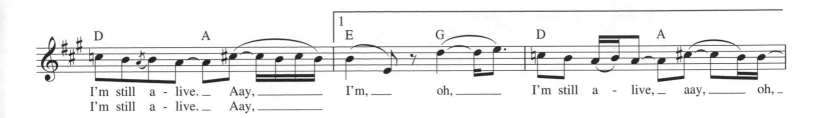

I'm still a - live.— Aay,_____ I'm,— oh,_____ I'm still a - live,_ aay,_____ oh,_

I'm still a - live.— Aay,_____

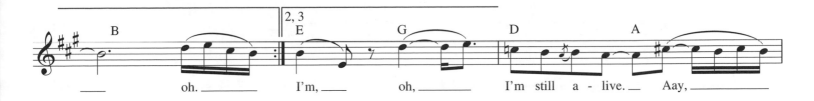

___ oh._____ I'm,___ oh,_____ I'm still a - live.— Aay,_____

I'm,— oh,_____ I'm still a - live,_ aay._____

I'm,— oo, I'm still a - live,_____ yeah, yeah, yeah, yeah, yeah, yeah.

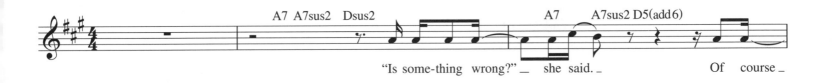

"Is some-thing wrong?"_ she said._____ Of course_

___ there is._ "You're_ still a - live," she said._____ Oh, and do I de - serve_

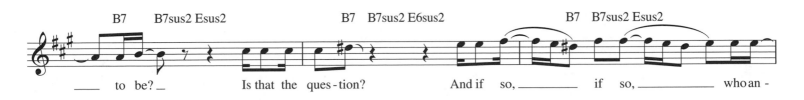

___ to be?_ Is that the ques-tion? And if so,_____ if so,_____ who an -

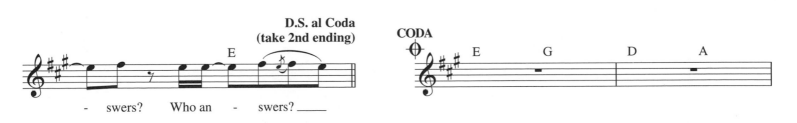

- swers? Who an - swers?_____

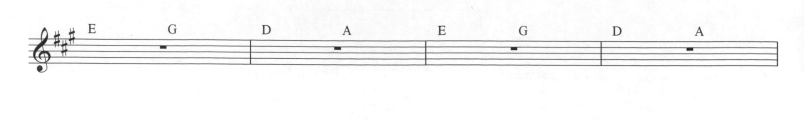

rit.

Any Way You Want It

Words and Music by Steve Perry and Neal Schon

- y way you want __ it.

- y way you want __ it.

She said, "Hold, _____

hold _____ on, __ hold _____ on, __ hold _____ on!" __

_____

Oh, __ she said, "An - y way you want it. That's the way you need __ it. An -

- y way you want __ it. An - y way! _____ An - y way you want it. That's

the way you need __ it. An - y way you want __ it." Oh, __ she said, "An -

Additional Lyrics

2. I was alone,
   I never knew
   What good love can do.
   Ooh, then we touched,
   Then we sang,
   About the lovin' things.
   Ooh, all night, all night,
   Oh, every night.
   So hold tight, hold tight,
   Oh, baby, hold tight.
   Chorus

Almost Easy

Words and Music by Matthew Sanders, James Sullivan, Brian Haner, Jr. and Zachary Baker

American Woman

Written by Burton Cummings, Randy Bachman, Gary Peterson and Jim Kale

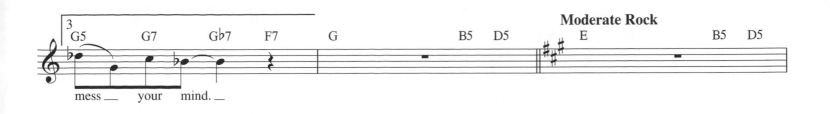

A-mer-i-can wom - an,   stay a-way from   me. _____   A-mer-i-can wom-
A-mer-i-can wom - an,   get-a-way from   me. _____   A-mer-i-can wom-
     - an,   I said get   a - way. _____   A-mer-i-can wom-

- an,   ma - ma,   let   me   be. _____
- an,   ma - ma,   let   me   be. _____
- an,   lis - ten   what   I   say. _____

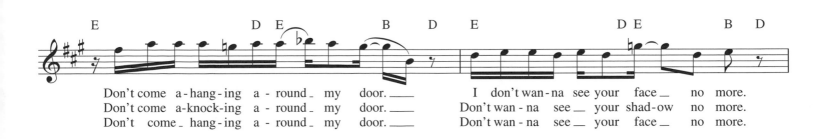

Don't come a-hang-ing a - round _ my   door. _____   I don't wan-na see your face _ no more.
Don't come a-knock-ing a - round _ my   door. _____   Don't wan-na   see _ your shad-ow   no more.
Don't come _ hang-ing a - round _ my   door. _____   Don't wan-na   see _ your face _ no more.

I got more im-por-tant things to   do _____   than spend my   time _ grow-ing old _ with you. _____ Now,
Col-ored lights   can hyp - no - tize. ___   Spar-kle some - one else - 's eyes. _____ Now,
I don't need _ your war ma - chines. _   I don't need _ your _ ghet - to scenes. _____

15

CODA

wom-an, ma-ma, let me be.

Go. Got-ta get a-way, got-ta get a-way now go, go, go. ___ I'm gon-na

leave you, wom-an. Gon-na leave you, wom-an. Bye, bye. ___ Bye,

bye. ___ Bye, bye. ___ Bye, bye. ___ You're ___

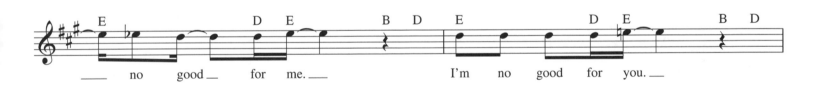

___ no good ___ for me. ___ I'm no good ___ for you. ___

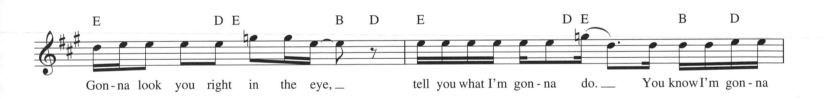

Gon-na look you right in the eye, ___ tell you what I'm gon-na do. ___ You know I'm gon-na

leave. You know I'm gon-na go. You know I'm gon-na

leave. I know I'm gon-na go, ___ wom-an. I'm gon-na...

Aqualung

Music by Ian Anderson
Lyrics by Jennie Anderson

Dee, _ dee, dee, dee, ___ dee, dee, dee, dee, _ dee, dee. _____

Dee, dee, dee, dee, dee, dee, ___ dee, dee, dee, dee. ___

Aq-ua-lung, my friend, _ don't you start a - way ___ un-eas - y. You

poor old sod, _ you see it's on - ly me, yeah. _

Hmm. _

D.S. al Coda

CODA

Whoa, oh, _____

oh, Aq - ua - lung. _____

Chop Suey!

Words and Music by Daron Malakian and Serj Tankian

fa-ble,   you want-ed to. Grab a brush and put a lit-tle make-up,   you want-ed to. Hide the scars to fade a-way the

shake up,   you want-ed to. Why'd you leave the keys up-on the ta-ble?   You want-ed to.   I   don't   think   you

trust   in   my   self - right - eous su - i -

cide. _   I   cry _   when   an - gels   de - serve   to _

die. _____

Rah! _____   die

in _____   my ___   self - right - eous su - i - cide. ___

I _____   cry ___   when   an - gels ___ de - serve   to   die.

Bodhisattva

Words and Music by Walter Becker and Donald Fagen

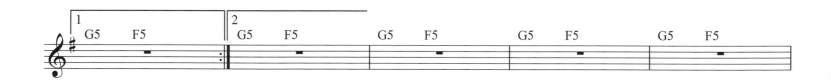

Carry On Wayward Son

Words and Music by Kerry Livgren

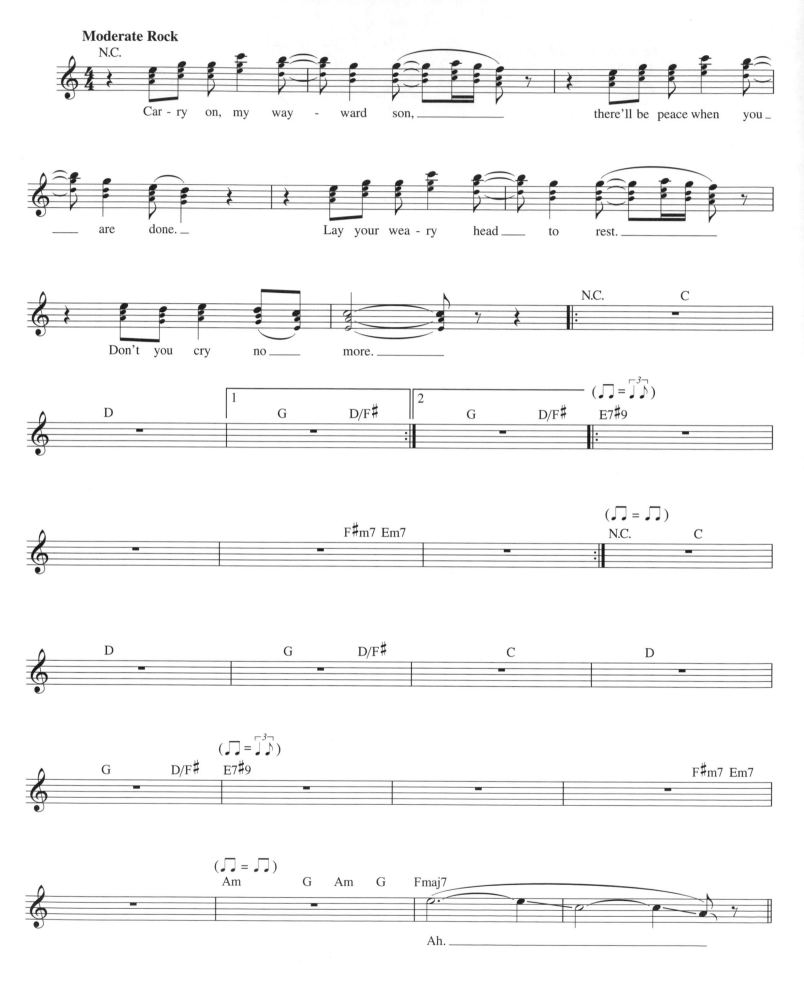

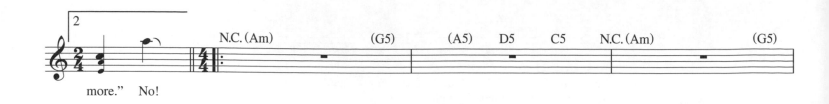

more." No!

Car - ry on, you will al - ways re - mem - ber. _____

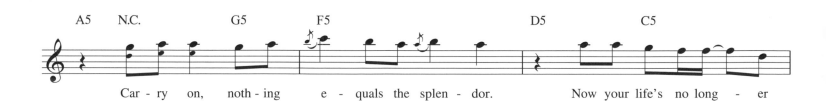

Car - ry on, noth - ing e - quals the splen - dor. Now your life's no long - er

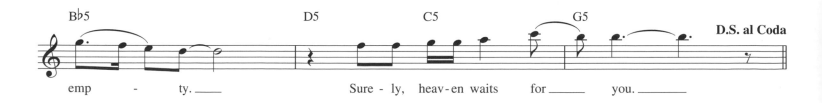

emp - ty. _____ Sure - ly, heav - en waits for _____ you. _____

D.S. al Coda

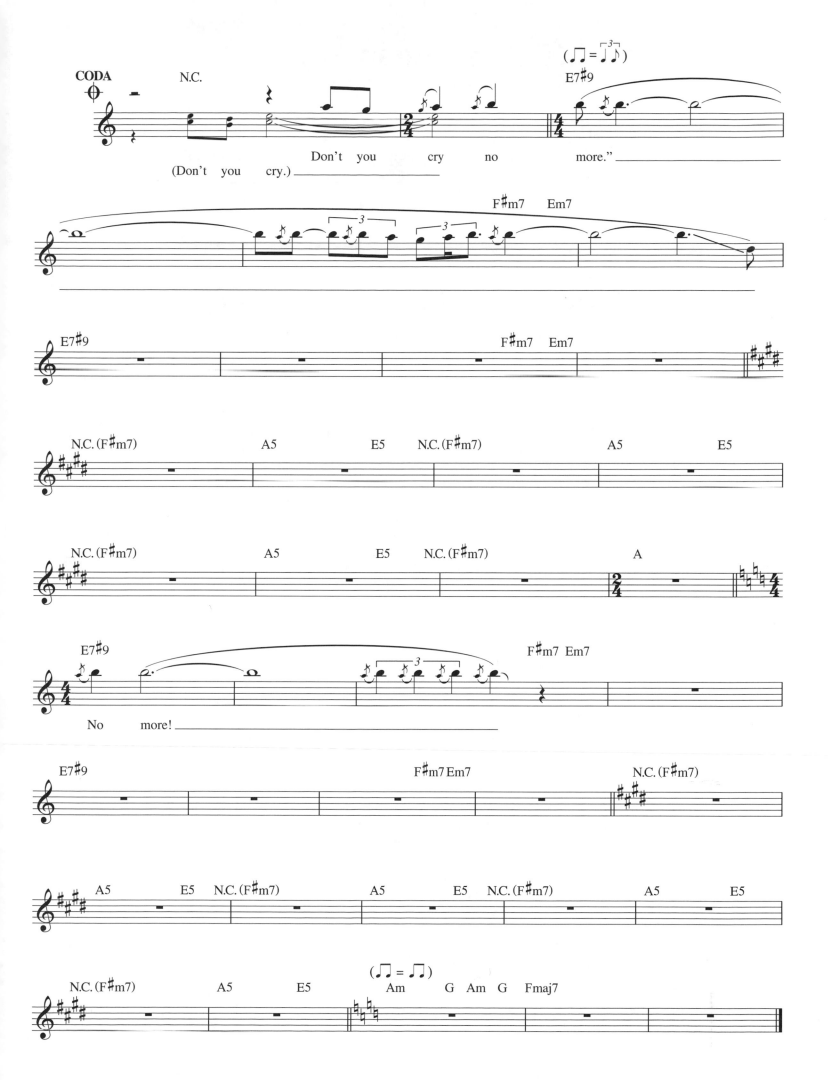

Come Out and Play

Words and Music by Dexter Holland

Moderately fast Rock

You got - ta keep 'em sep - a - rat - ed.

Like the lat - est fash - ion,
By the time you hear the si - ren,

like a spread-ing dis - ease. _____
it's al - read - y too late.

The kids are strap-pin' on their
One goes to the morgue and the

Down with the Sickness

Words and Music by Mike Wengren, Dan Donegan, Dave Draiman and Steve Kmak

chang - es, ____ vi - o - lent - ly it chang - es. ____ Oh, no. There _
chang - es, ____ liv - ing with these chang - es. ____ Oh, no. The

____ is ____ no turn - ing ____ back ____ now. You've wok - en up the
world is ____ a scar - y ____ place ____ now that you've wok - en up the

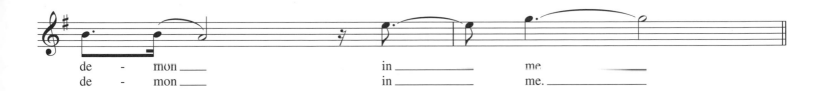

de - mon ____ in ____ me.
de - mon ____ in ____ me. ____

E5   F5 E5   F5 E5   F5 E5   F5 E5

Get up,   come on, get down _ with the sick - ness.   Get up,   come on, get down _ with the sick - ness.

F5 E5   F5 E5   F5 E5

Get up,   come on, get down _ with the sick - ness. _   O - pen up   your   hate   and let it flow in - to me.

F5 E5   F5 E5   F5 E5   F5 E5

Get up,   come on, get down _ with the sick - ness. You moth - er, get up,   come on, get down _ with the sick - ness. You

F5 E5   F5 E5 |1   F5 E5   F5 E5

fuck - er, get up,   come on, get down _ with the sick - ness. Mad - ness is ____ the   gift   that has been giv - en to me.

|2   F5 E5   F5 E5

Mad - ness is ____ the   gift   that has been giv - en to me.

And when I dream.

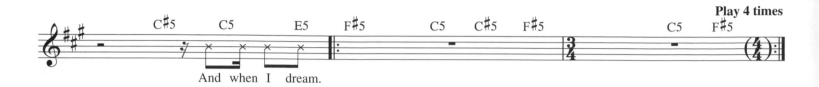

And when I dream.

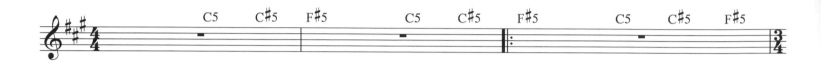

Get up, come on, get down with the sick - ness. Get up, come on, get down with the sick - ness.

Get up, come on, get down with the sick - ness. O - pen up your hate and let it flow in - to me.

Get up, come on, get down with the sick-ness. You moth-er, get up, come on, get down with the sick-ness. You

fuck-er, get up, come on, get down with the sick - ness. Mad-ness has now come o - ver me.

Drain You

Words and Music by Kurt Cobain

One ba - by to ____ an-oth - er says ____ I'm luck - y ____ to have met ____ you.

I don't ____ care what ____ you think ____ un - less ____ it is ____ a - bout ____ me.

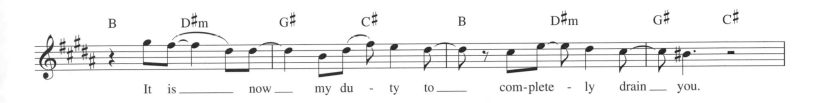

It is ____ now ____ my du - ty to ____ com - plete - ly drain ____ you.

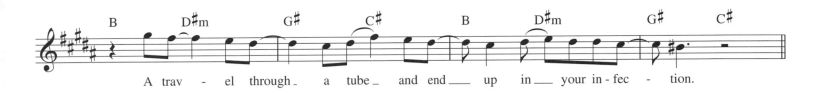

A trav - el through ____ a tube ____ and end ____ up in ____ your in - fec - tion.

Chew your meat for you, ____ pass it ____ back and forth ____

To Coda I ⊕
To Coda II ⊕

in a ____ pas - sion - ate kiss ____ from my ____ mouth to yours. ____

I like you. With eyes ____ so di -

Screamed: Ah! _____

One ba - by to _____ an - oth - er says _____ I'm luck - y to have

met you. I don't _ care what _____ you think _ un - less _____ it is _ a - bout _

_____ me. It is _____ now _ my du - ty to _ com-plete - ly drain _

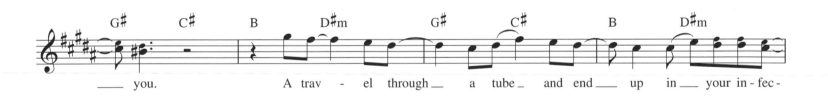

_____ you. A trav - el through _ a tube _ and end _ up in _ your in - fec -

D.S. al Coda II　　　**CODA II**

- tion. Slop-py _ lips to lips. _____ You're my _

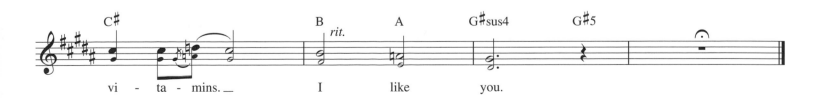

vi - ta - mins. _ I like you.

E-Pro

Words and Music by Beck, Mike Simpson, John King, Michael Diamond, Adam Horovitz and Adam Yauch

good in us __ (is) all we know. There's too much left to taste __ that's bit - ter.

I won't give up that ghost. __ It's sick the way __ these tongues are twist - ed. The

good in us __ (is) all we know. There's too much left to taste __ that's bit - ter.

E5   D5   C5   A5   E5   D5   C5   A5

Nah, nah,   nah, nah, nah, nah,   nah.   Nah, nah,   nah, nah, nah, nah,   nah.

E5   D5   C5   A5   E5   D5   C5   A5

Nah, nah,   nah, nah, nah, nah,   nah.   Nah, nah,   nah, nah, nah, nah,   nah.

E5   D5   C5   A5   E5   D5   C5   A5

Nah, nah,   nah, nah, nah, nah,   nah.   Nah, nah,   nah, nah, nah, nah,   nah.

(Nah, nah, yeah, __ yeah.) _____

E5   D5   C5   A5   E5   D5   C5

Nah, nah,   nah, nah, nah, nah,   nah.   Nah, nah,   nah, nah, nah, nah,

_____

A5   E5   D5   C5   A5   **Play 3 times**   E5   D5   C5

nah.   Nah, nah,   nah, nah, nah, nah,

A5   E5   D5   C5   A5   **Play 4 times**   A5

nah.

Everlong

Words and Music by David Grohl

Moderately fast Rock

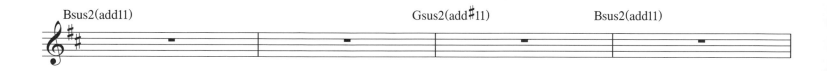

Hel - lo, _____ I've wait - ed here _____ for you
Come _____ down _____ and waste a - way _____ with me,
Breathe _____ out _____ so I can breathe _____ you in, _____

ev - er - long. ____
down with ____ me ____
hold you ____ in. ____

To - night ____ I've thrown my - self in - to ____
slow, ____ how ____ you want - ed it to be. ____
And ____ now ____ I know you've al - ways been

and out of the red, ____ out of her head ____ she sang. ____
I'm o - ver my head, ____ out of her head ____ she sang. ____
out of your head, ____ out of my head ____ I sang. ____

And I ____ won - der,

when I sing a - long ____ with you, ____

if ev - 'ry - thing could ev - er feel this real ____ for - ev - er,
Sing vocal harmony 2nd and 3rd times only.

if an - y - thing could ev - er be this good ____ { (1.) a -
{ (2.,3.) a -

- gain.
- gain.

The on - ly thing I'll ev - er

45

D5   A5   **To Coda II** ⊕

ask of you: ___ you've got to prom - ise not to stop when I ___ say ___

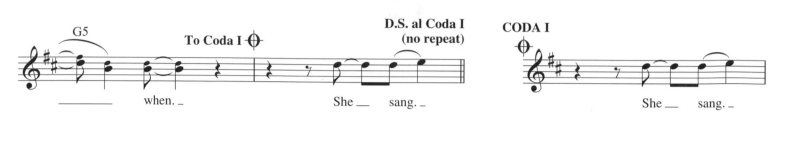

G5   **To Coda I** ⊕   **D.S. al Coda I**   **CODA I**

(no repeat)

___ when. ___ She __ sang. ___ She __ sang. ___

Dmaj7(add9)

Bsus2(add11)   Gsus2(add♯11)

Bsus2(add11)   N.C.(D)

And ___ I _____ won - der

D.S.S. al Coda II   **CODA II**

B5   G5

___ when. ___

Eye of the Tiger

Theme from ROCKY III

Words and Music by Frank Sullivan and Jim Peterik

eye of the ti - ger, it's the thrill of the fight, ris - ing up to the chal-lenge of our

ri - val. And __ the last known sur-vi - vor stalks his prey in the night, and __ he's

watch-in' us all with the eye of the ti - ger.

D.S. al Coda

CODA

eye _____ of the ti -

- ger.

The eye of the ti - ger.

The eye of the ti - ger. __

The eye of the ti - ger. __

The eye of the ti - ger. __

Feel the Pain

Words and Music by Joseph Mascis, Jr.

CODA

Hey, __ now, take __ it back. __

Get __ off the __ at - tack. __

Trail - ing on __ your scene. __

Just try ___ and keep __ it clean. _____

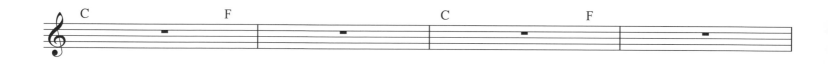

Float On

Words and Music by Isaac Brock, Eric Judy and Dann Gallucci

right, don't _ wor - ry we'll all float on. _____

(Al - right al - read - y.)

And we'll all _

_____ float on. Al - right al - read - y, we'll all _____ float _ on. Al -

right, don't wor - ry e - ven if things end up a bit too heav - y. We'll all _

_ float _ on. Al - right al - read - y, we'll all _____ float on. Al -

right al - read - y, we'll all _____ float _ on O. K. Don't wor - ry, we'll all _

_ float on. E - ven if things get heav - y, we'll _ all _____ float _ on. Al -

right al - read - y, we'll all float on all.... Don't you wor - ry, we'll

(All, al - right.)

all float on. _ We'll all float on. _____

Al - right.)

Give It Away

Words and Music by Anthony Kiedis, Flea, John Frusciante and Chad Smith

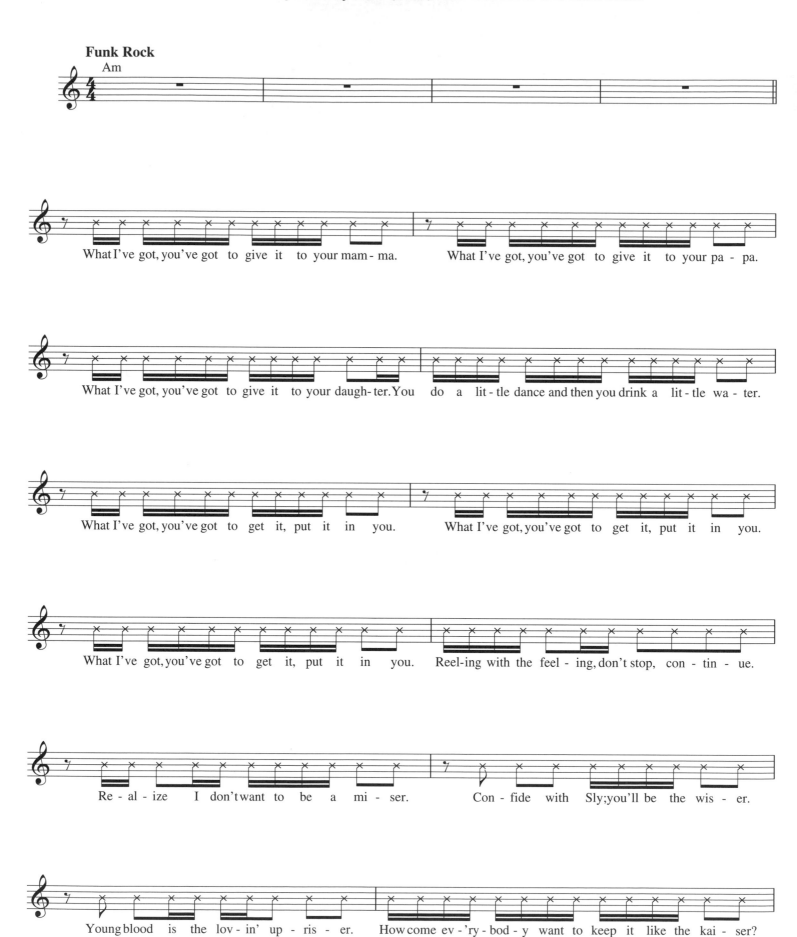

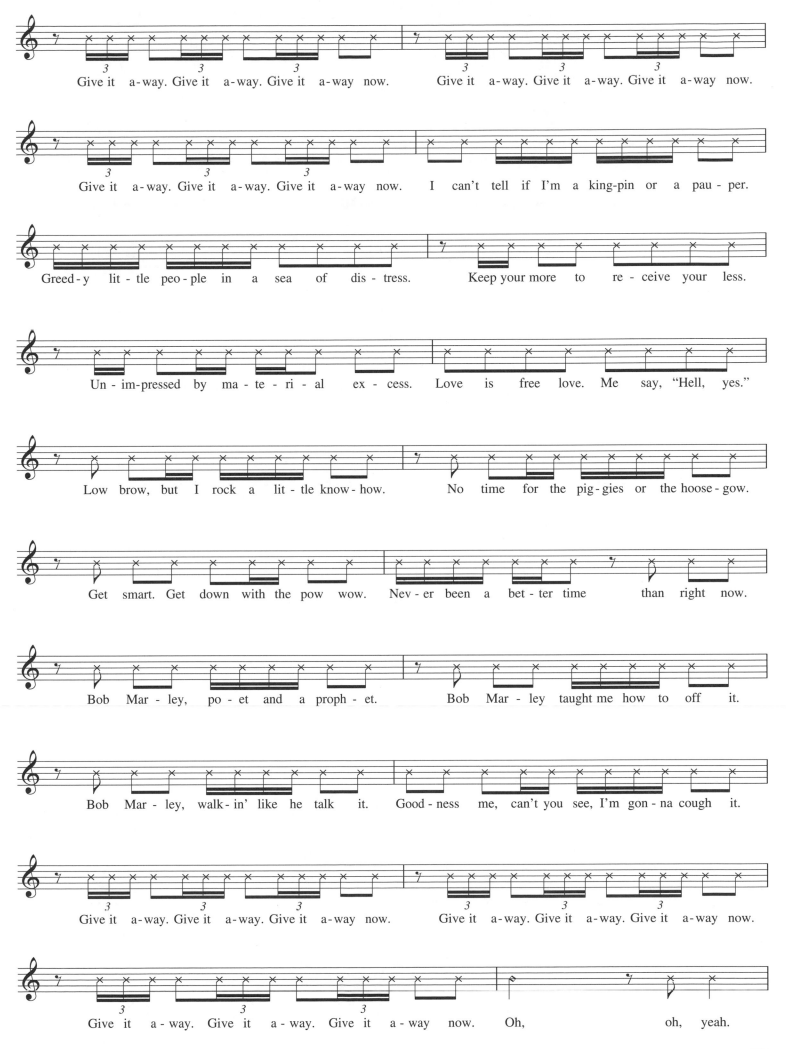

Give it a-way. Give it a-way. Give it a-way now. Give it a-way. Give it a-way. Give it a-way now.

Give it a-way. Give it a-way. Give it a-way now. I can't tell if I'm a king-pin or a pau-per.

Greed-y lit-tle peo-ple in a sea of dis-tress. Keep your more to re-ceive your less.

Un-im-pressed by ma-te-ri-al ex-cess. Love is free love. Me say, "Hell, yes."

Low brow, but I rock a lit-tle know-how. No time for the pig-gies or the hoose-gow.

Get smart. Get down with the pow wow. Nev-er been a bet-ter time than right now.

Bob Mar-ley, po-et and a proph-et. Bob Mar-ley taught me how to off it.

Bob Mar-ley, walk-in' like he talk it. Good-ness me, can't you see, I'm gon-na cough it.

Give it a-way. Give it a-way. Give it a-way now. Give it a-way. Give it a-way. Give it a-way now.

Give it a-way. Give it a-way. Give it a-way now. Oh, oh, yeah.

Give it a-way. Give it a-way. Give it a-way now. Give it a-way. Give it a-way. Give it a-way now.

Give it a-way. Give it a-way. Give it a-way now. I can't tell if I'm a king-pin or a pau-per.

Em

1

2

Luck-y

Am

me, swim-min' in my a-bil-i-ty. ___ Danc-in' down on life with a-gil-i-ty. Come and

drink it up from my fer-til-i-ty. ___ Blessed with a buck-et of luck-y mo-bil-i-ty.

My mom, I love her 'cause she love me. Long gone are the times when she scrub me.

Feel-in' good, my broth-er gon-na bug me. Drink-in' my juice, young love, chug-a-lug me.

There's a riv-er born to be a giv-er. Keep you warm, won't let you shiv-er.

His heart is nev-er gon-na with-er. Come on, ev-'ry-bod-y, time to de-liv-er.

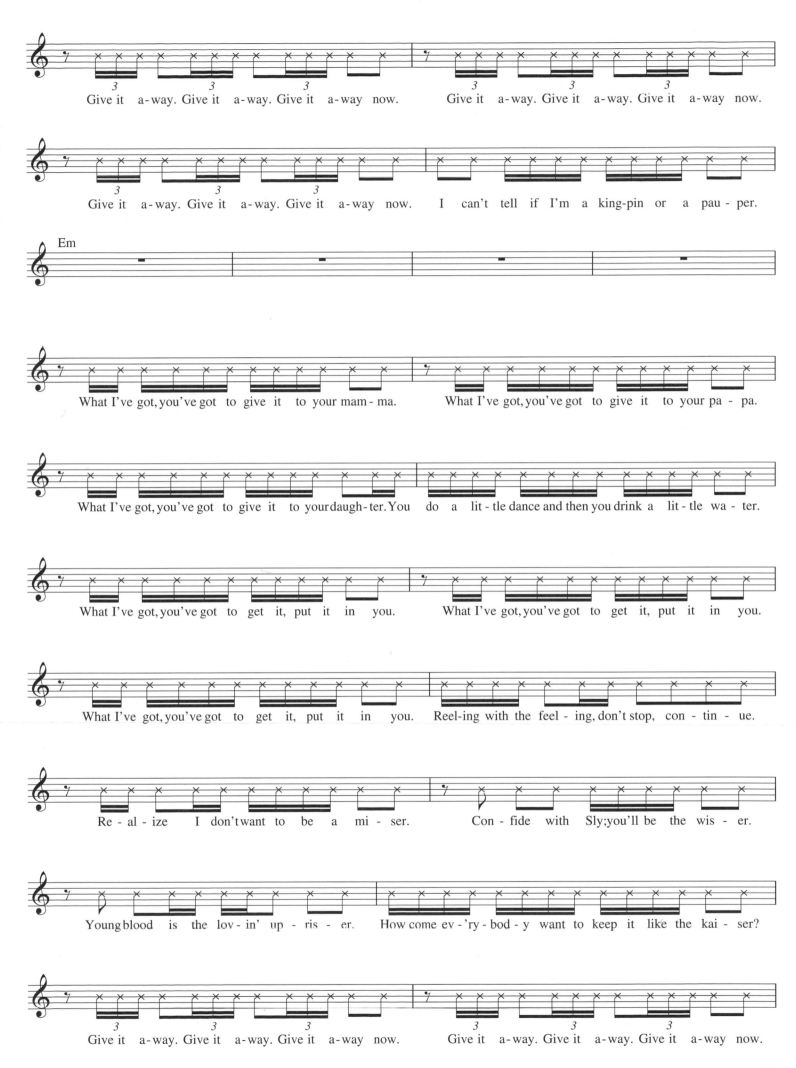

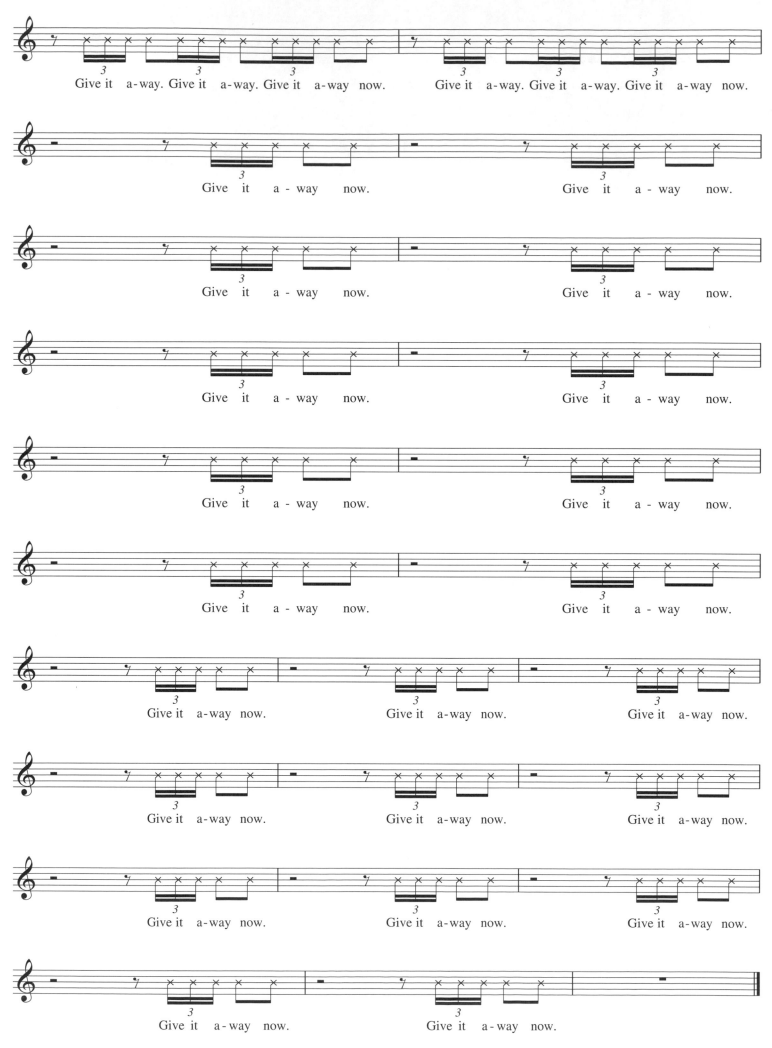

Go Your Own Way

Words and Music by Lindsey Buckingham

D.S. al Coda II

CODA II

your own way.

You can call it an-oth - er lone-ly day.

You can go your own way.

You can call

it an-oth - er lone-ly day.

You can go your own way.

63

I Was Wrong

Words and Music by Michael Ness

Self - de - struc - tion's got me a - gain. I was wrong. ____

I re - al - ized __ now that I was wrong. __ An' I

I was wrong. __ I was wrong. ____ yeah! ____

Oo, I __ was wrong. ____ I

grew up fast, __ I grew up hard. __ Some - thing was wrong __ from the

ver - y start. __ I was fight - in' ev - 'ry - bod - y, ____ I was __

__ fight - in' ev - 'ry - thing. But the on - ly one ____ that I

hurt was me. __ I got so - ci - et - y's blood run - nin' down my face. __

Some - bod - y help __ me get out - ta this place. __ How could some - one's bad

luck last so _____ long? Un - til I _____ re - al-ized that I was so _____ wrong. _____

Oo, I _____ was

CODA

I was wrong. _____ I was wrong. _____

Self - de - struc - tion's got me a - gain. _____ I was wrong. _____

The on - ly _____ one _____ that I hurt was _____ me.

Well, I was wrong. _____

Peace Sells

Words and Music by Dave Mustaine

Moderate Rock

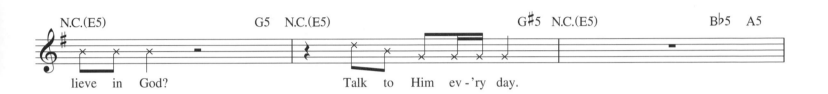

What do you mean I don't be -

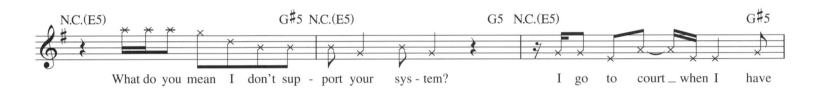

lieve in God? Talk to Him ev -'ry day.

What do you mean I don't sup - port your sys - tem? I go to court _ when I have

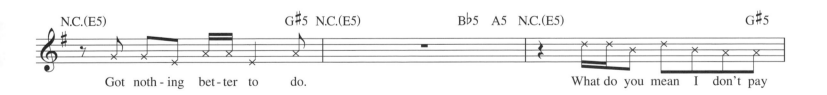

to. What do you mean I can't get to work on time?

Got noth - ing bet - ter to do. What do you mean I don't pay

my bills? Why do you think I'm broke? Huh?

If there's a new _ way,

well, I'll be the first _ in line.

But it bet-ter work this time. _

_

What do you mean I hurt your feel-ings? _

I did-n't know you had an-y _ feel-

ings.

What do you mean I ain't kind? ___

Just not your kind.

What do you mean I could-n't

be the Pres - i - dent

of the U - ni - ted States of A - mer -

i - ca?

Tell me some-thing,

it's still "We, _

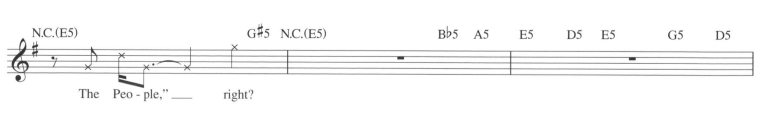

The Peo - ple," ___ right?

If there's a new way, well, I'll be the first in line.

But it bet-ter work this time.

Oh.

Can you put a price on peace?

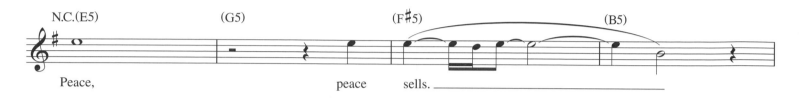

Peace,   peace sells. _____

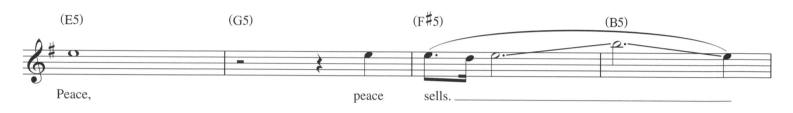

Peace,   peace sells. _____

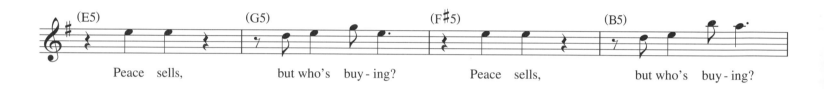

Peace sells,   but who's buy-ing?   Peace sells,   but who's buy-ing?

Peace sells,   but who's buy-ing?   Peace sells,   but who's buy-ing?

Peace sells,   but who's buy-ing?   Peace sells,   but who's buy-ing?

(E5)   (G5)   (F#5)   (B5)

Peace sells,   but who's buy-ing?   Peace sells,   but who's buy-ing?

(E5)   (G5)   (F#5)   (B5)

Peace sells,   but who's buy-ing?   Peace sells,   but who's buy-ing?

(E5)   (G5)   (F#5)   (B5)   G#5 G5

Peace sells,   but who's buy-ing?   Peace sells,   but who's buy-ing?

F#5 F5 E5 F5 F#5 F5 E5 F#5 G5   F#5   G5 F#5 N.C.(F#5)

No, ___   no, no, no,   no. _____

(B5)   G#5 G5 F#5 F5 E5 F5 F#5 F5 E5 F#5   G5   F#5   G5 F#5

Peace   sells. _____   (Ah.) _____

N.C.(F#5)   (B5)   G#5 G5 F#5 F5 E5 F5 F#5 F5 E5 F#5

G5   F#5   G5 F#5 N.C.(F#5)   (B5)   G#5   G5

Peace

F#5 F5 E5 F5 F#5 F5 E5 F#5   G5   F#5   G5 F#5   E5

sells. _____   Ah!

Let There Be Rock

Words and Music by Ronald Scott, Angus Young and Malcolm Young

'n' there was drums. "Let there be gui-

-tar," there was gui - tar. Let there be rock.

A5

(Vocal 1st time only)

B5

Freely
A7 A7sus4   E7#9 (G5)*E5   A5
A5

play on repeats only

E5   G5   E5 A5 E5 G5   E5 **Play 4 times**   N.C.
And it came _ to pass, _

_ that Rock 'n' Roll _ was born. _ All a - cross the land, _ ev - 'ry

rock- in' band, _ was blow- in' up a storm. And the gui - tar man _ got fa -

mous, the bus'-ness - man __ got rich. __ And in ev -'ry bar __ there was a

su - per-star, with a sev-en year itch. __ There were fif - teen mil - lion fin -

- gers learn-in' how __ to play. And you could hear the fin - gers pick - in', __

__ and this is what they __ had to say: __ Let there be light, __

sound, drums,

A5

gui - tar, ow! "Let there be rock." __

(Vocal 1st time only)

B5

A5   G5

Livin' on a Prayer

Words and Music by Jon Bon Jovi, Desmond Child and Richie Sambora

hold __ on __ to what we've got. It does-n't make a dif-f'rence if we make it or not. We've

got each oth - er, and that's a lot for __ love. __ We'll give it a shot.

Whoa, _____ we're half - way __ there. __ Oh, _____ liv - in' on a prayer. __

Take my __ hand, _ we'll make it, I swear. _ Oh, _____ liv - in' on a prayer.

1
Em

2
C5
Liv - in' on __ a prayer. _____

Oo, _____ we've got to

hold __ on, _ read-y or __ not. You live for the fight when that's all that you've got.

Whoa, _____ we're half - way there. _ Whoa, _____ liv - in' on a prayer. __

Play 3 times and Fade

Take my hand _ and we'll make it, I swear. _ Whoa, _____ liv - in' on a prayer. _

Lump

Words and Music by Chris Ballew, Dave Dederer and Jason Finn

Man in the Box

Written by Jerry Cantrell, Layne Staley, Sean Kinney and Michael Starr

Mountain Song

Words and Music by Jane's Addiction

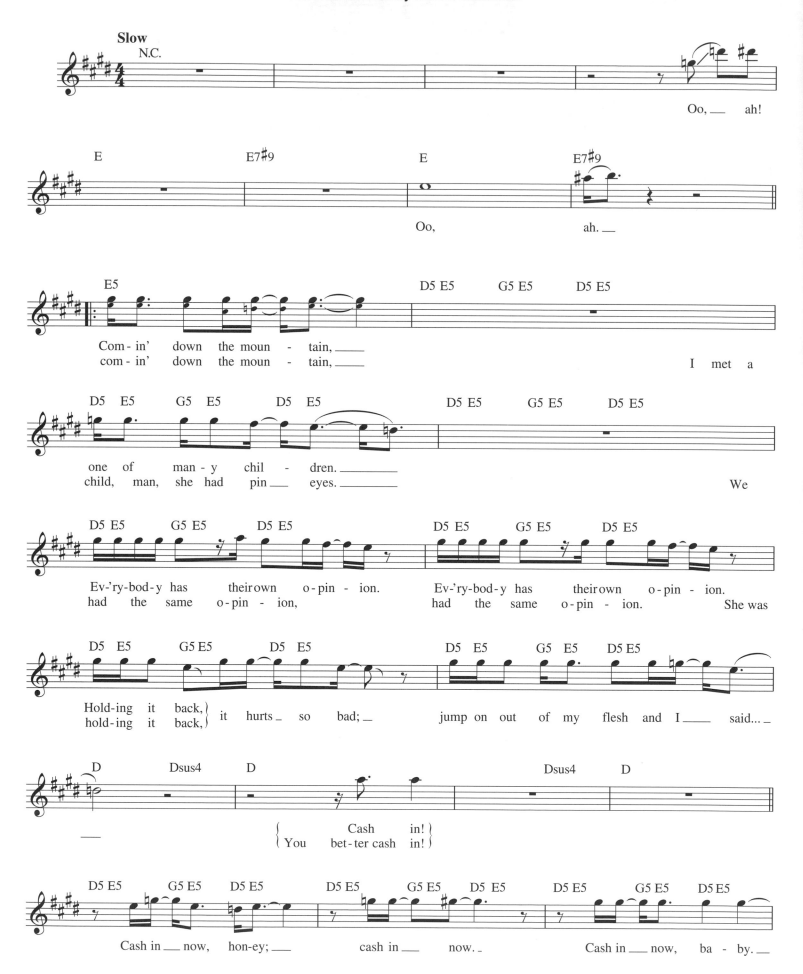

My Own Worst Enemy

Words and Music by Jeremy Popoff, Jay Popoff, Kevin Baldes and Allen Shellenberger

To Coda ⊕

F#5

I came in through the win - dow ___ last night and you're ___ gone,

1 E5

B5 A5 E5

gone. ___

2 E5

B5 A5

___ gone,

B5 A5 E5

gone. ___

B5 A5 E5

D.S. al Coda

B5 A5 E5

B5 A5

Please tell me

CODA ⊕

B5/F#

night. ___

(Ah,

E5

F#5

It's no sur - prise ___ to me, ___ I am ___ my own ___ worst en - e - my. ___

hoo.

Ah,

A5

B5/F#

'Cause ev - 'ry now ___ and then ___ I kick ___ the liv - in' shit out - ta me. ___

hoo. ___

Ah,

E5

F#5

Can we for - get ___ a - bout ___ the things ___ I said ___ when I ___ was drunk? ___

hoo. ___

Ah,

A5

B5/F#

I did - n't mean ___ to call ___ you that. ___

hoo.) ___

E5

B5 A5 E5

B5 A5

One Step Closer

Words and Music by Rob Bourdon, Brad Delson, Joe Hahn, Mike Shinoda and Charles Bennington

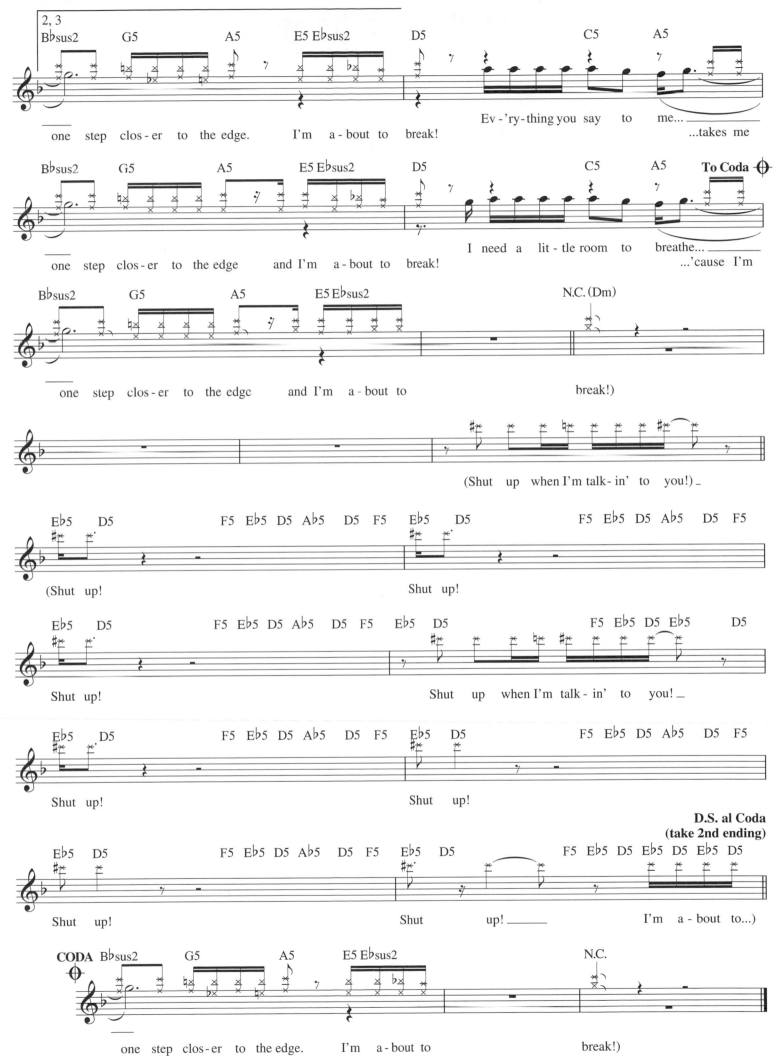

One Way or Another

Words and Music by Deborah Harry and Nigel Harrison

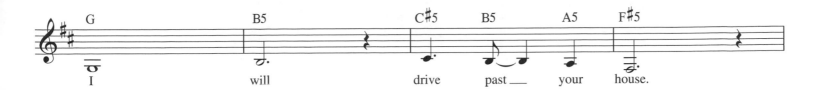

G   B5   C#5   B5   A5   F#5

I   will   drive   past ___ your   house.

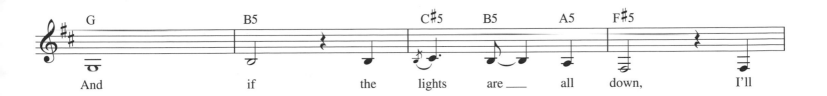

G   B5   C#5   B5   A5   F#5

And   if   the   lights   are ___ all   down,   I'll

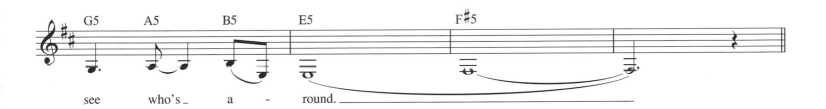

G5   A5   B5   E5   F#5

see   who's _ a - round. _____

D5   D   C#5 C5 B5

One   way   or an - oth - er,   I'm gon-na   find ya.   I'm gon-na   get ya, get ya, get ya, get ya.

B   C5 C#5 D5

One   way _   or an - oth - er,   I'm gon-na   win ya.   I'll   get ya,   I'll get ya.

D   C#5 C5 B5

One   way   or an - oth - er,   I'm gon-na   see ya.   I'm gon-na   meet ya, meet ya, meet ya, meet ya.

B

One   day, _   may-be next week,   I'm gon-na   meet ya.   I'll   meet ya,   ah. ___

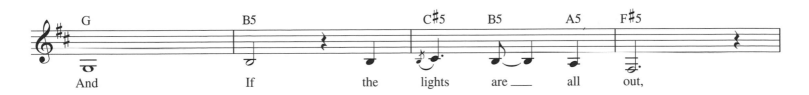

G   B5   C#5   B5   A5   F#5

And   If   the   lights   are ___ all   out,

One way or an - oth - er, I'm gon - na lose ya. I'm gon - na give you the slip.

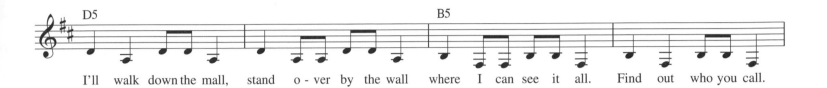

I'll walk down the mall, stand o - ver by the wall where I can see it all. Find out who you call.

Lead you to the su - per - mar - ket, check out some spe - cials and rap. We'd get lost in the crowd.

Where I can see it all, find out who you call.

(One way __ or an - oth - er, I'm gon - na get ya. I'll get ya, I'll get ya, get ya, get ya, get ya.

Where I can see it all, find out who you call.

One way __ or an - oth - er, I'm gon - na get ya. I'll get ya, I'll get ya, get ya, get ya, get ya.

Where I can see it all, find out who you call.

One way __ or an - oth - er, I'm gon - na get ya. I'll get ya, I'll get ya, get ya, get ya, get ya.

Play 3 times and Fade

Where I can see it all, find out who you call.

One way __ or an - oth - er, I'm gon - na get ya. I'll get ya, I'll get ya, get ya, get ya, get ya.)

Pinball Wizard

Words and Music by Peter Townshend

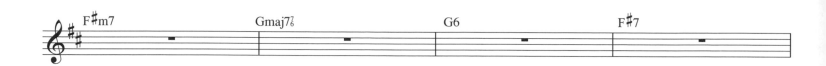

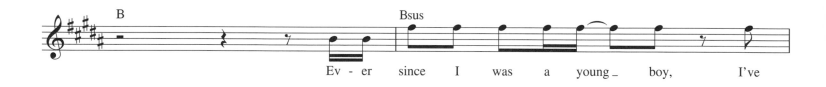

Ev - er since I was a young _ boy, I've

played the sil - ver ball. _ From So - ho down to Brigh - ton, I

must - 've played 'em all. _____ But I ain't seen noth - in' like _ him in

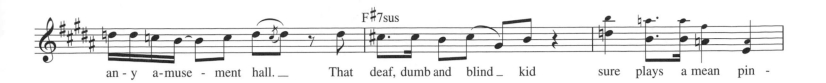
an-y a-muse-ment hall. ___ That deaf, dumb and blind ___ kid sure plays a mean pin -

ball.

He stands like a stat - ue, be-comes part of the ma - chine. ___

Feel - in' all ___ the bump - ers, al - ways play-ing clean. ___

Plays by in - tu - i - tion, the dig - it count-ers fall. ___ That

deaf, dumb and blind ___ kid sure plays a mean pin - ball.

He's a

pin - ball wiz - ard. There has ___ to be a twist. A pin - ball wiz-ard's got

such a sup - ple wrist. ____

How do you think __ he does __ it?
(I don't __ know.) _____
What makes him __ so

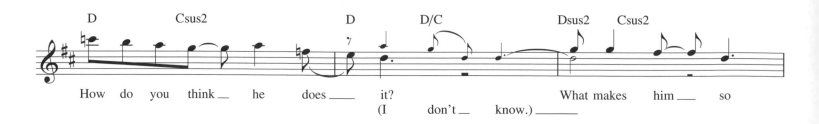

good? _
Ain't got no dis - trac - tions, can't hear no buz - zers and bells. Don't

see no lights a - flash - in', plays by sense of smell. __

Al - ways gets a re - play, nev - er seen __ him fall. ____ That

deaf, dumb and blind __ kid sure plays a mean pin - ball.

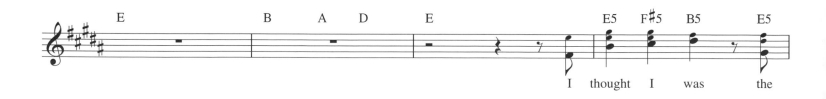

I thought I was the

Bal - ly ta - ble king, but I just hand - ed my pin - ball crown to

him. _____

E - ven   on   my   fa - v'rite   ta - ble,

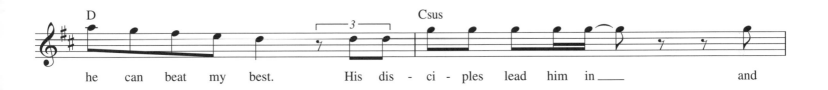

he   can   beat   my   best.   His   dis - ci - ples   lead   him   in ____   and

he   just   does   the   rest. ____   He's   got   cra - zy   flip - per   fin - gers,

nev - er   seen   him   fall. __   That   deaf, dumb and blind __ kid   sure   plays   a   mean   pin -

ball.

Ramblin' Man

Words and Music by Dickey Betts

Rock'n Me

Words and Music by Steve Miller

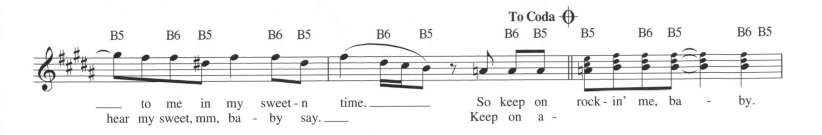

to me in my sweet-n time._____ So keep on rock-in' me, ba - by.
hear my sweet, mm, ba - by say.____ Keep on a -

Keep on a - rock-in' me, ba - by. Keep on a -

rock-in' me, ba - by. Keep on a - rock-in' me, ba - by.

I went from Phoe-nix, Ar - i - zo - na all the way to Ta - co - ma, Phil - a -

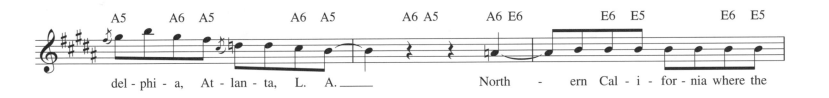

del - phi - a, At - lan - ta, L. A.____ North - ern Cal - i - for - nia where the

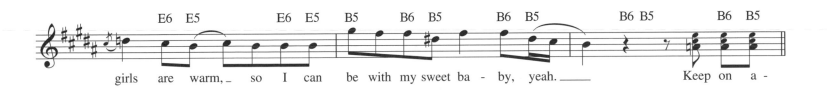

girls are warm,_ so I can be with my sweet ba - by, yeah.____ Keep on a -

rock-in' me, ba - by. Keep on a - rock-in' me, ba - by.

Keep on a - rock-in' me, ba - by. Keep on a -

rock-in' me, ba - by. Baby, ba-by, baby, keep on rock-in',

rock-in' me, __ ba - by. Keep on a-

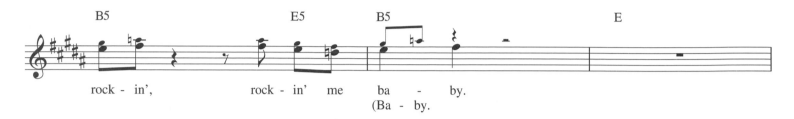

rock-in', rock-in' me ba - by.
(Ba - by.

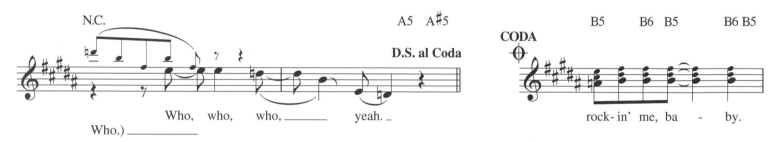

D.S. al Coda **CODA**

Who, who, who, _____ yeah. __ rock-in' me, ba - by.
Who.) _____

Keep on a-rock-in' me, ba - by. Keep on a-

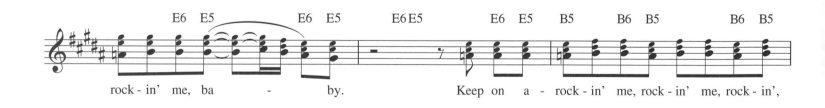

rock-in' me, ba - by. Keep on a-rock-in' me, rock-in' me, rock-in',

ba-by, ba-by, ba-by. Keep on rock-in' me, ba - by. Keep on a-

rock-in' me, ba - by. Keep on a-rock-in' me, ba - by.

Round and Round

Words and Music by Robbin Lantz Crosby, Warren DeMartini and Stephen E. Pearcy

Shooting Star

Words and Music by Paul Rodgers

Moderately slow

John-ny was a school-boy when he heard his first Bea-tle song. ___

"Love Me Do," ___ I think it was, and from there ___ it did-n't take him long. ___

Got him-self a gui-tar, used to play ev-er-y night. ___

Now he's in a rock 'n' roll out-fit and ev-er-y-thing's ___ all ___ right. Don't you know? ___

John-ny told his ma-ma, ___ "Hey, ___

Ma-ma, I'm ___ go-in' a-way. ___ I'm gon-na hit the big time, ___ gon-na

be a big star some-day, yeah." Ma-ma came to the door with a tear-

-drop in her eye. Johnny said, "Don't cry, Ma-ma,

smile and wave good-bye." Don't you know? Yeah,

yeah. Don't you know that you are a shoot-ing star? Don't you know?

Don't you know? Don't you know that you are a

shoot-ing star? And all the world will love you just as

long, as long as you are.

To Coda

John-ny made a rec-ord, went

straight up to num-ber one. Sud-den-ly ev-'ry-one loved to

hear __ him sing the song. ____ Watch-ing the world __ go by, ____ sur-

pris-ing it goes __ so fast. __ John-ny looked a-round him and said, __ "Well, I

made the big __ time at last." Don't you know? ____ Don't you know? __

__ Don't you __ know that you are a ____ shoot-ing star? Don't you

know? Whoa, ____ yeah. ____ Don't you __ know that you are a ____

shoot-ing star? ____ Yeah. ____ And all ____ the world __ will love __ you __ just as

long, ____ as long as you __ are ____ a shoot-ing star.

Don't you __

Spoonman

Words and Music by Chris Cornell

I'm to-geth - er with your plan. Save me, yeah.

(1.) A - save,

(2.,3.) A-

uh.

save,

Oh.

Well,

a - save

me.

Save me, yeah.

Save,

a - with your...

Come on, come on, come on.

Play 4 times

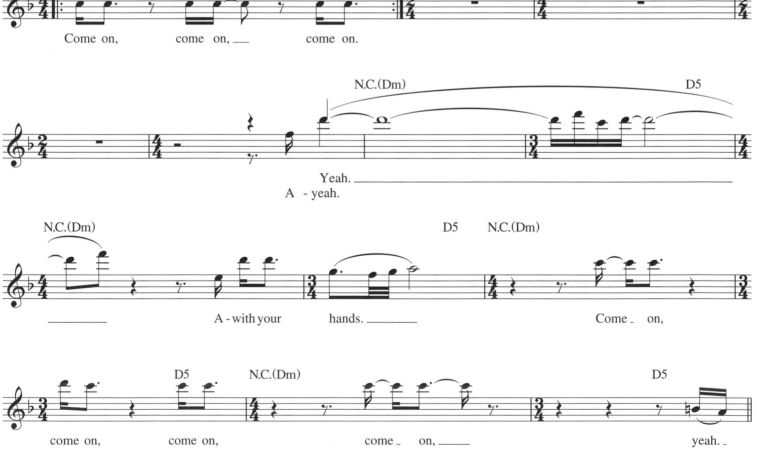

Yeah.

A - yeah.

A - with your hands.

Come on,

come on, come on,

come on, yeah.

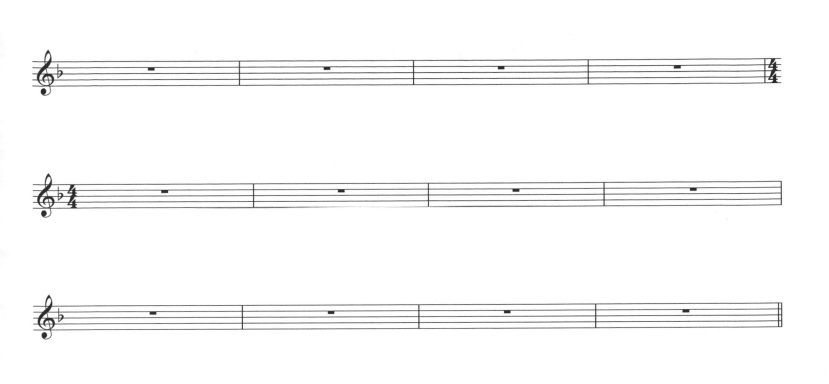

Play 7 times ... D.S. al Coda

Come on, we like it all. ___ Come on, we like it all. ___

CODA N.C.(Dm) D5

save, _____ yeah. _____ A-

N.C.(Dm) D5 N.C.(Dm)

save me, _____ yeah. A-with your, a-with your

D5 N.C.(Dm) G5

hands. Feel ___ the rhy - thm with ___ your hands, _____

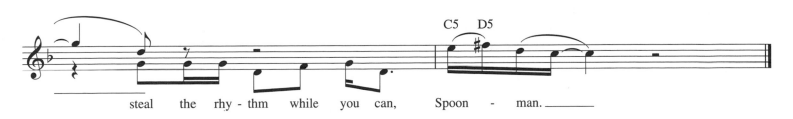

C5 D5

_____ steal the rhy - thm while you can, Spoon - man. ___

Spirit in the Sky

Words and Music by Norman Greenbaum

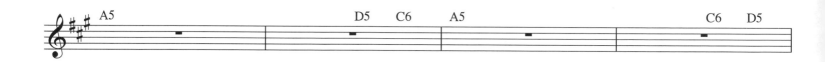

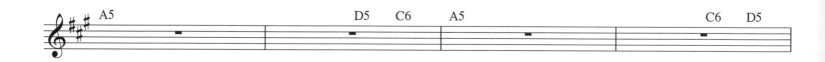

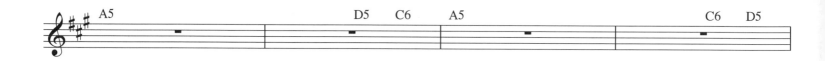

When I die and they lay me to rest, ___ gon - na go ___ to the place ___

___ that's the best. ___ When I lay me down ___ to die, ___ go - in' up ___

___ to the Spir - it in the Sky. Go - in' up ___ to the Spir -

go to the place _ that's the best.

Nev - er been a sin - ner, I nev - er sin. I got a friend in Je -
(I got a friend _ in Je -

- sus _____ so you know that when I die, _____ He's
- sus _____

gon - na set me up with the Spir - it in the Sky. Whoa, ___ set me up with the Spir -

it in the Sky. ___ That's where I'm gon-na go when I die. ___
(Spir - it in the Sky. _____ When I

___ When I die and they lay me to rest, ___ I'm gon - na go to the place ___ that's the
die.)

best. Go to the place ___ that's the best.

The Trees

Words by Neil Peart
Music by Geddy Lee and Alex Lifeson

Lyrics:

There is un-rest in the for-est. There is trou-ble with the trees. For the ma-ples want more sun-light and the oaks ig-nore their pleas.

The

So the trees are all kept e - qual by

hatch - et, axe, and saw.

White Wedding

Words and Music by Billy Idol

nice day to start a - gain. It's a

To Coda ⊕

nice day for a white wed - ding. It's a

1.
nice day to start a - gain.

2.
nice day to start a - gain, ow!

Pick it up.

D.S. al Coda

Take me back home, yeah.

123

We Got the Beat

Words and Music by Charlotte Caffey

You Oughta Know

Lyrics by Alanis Morissette
Music by Alanis Morissette and Glen Ballard

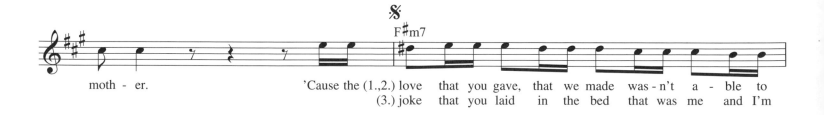

- -'ry time you speak her name does she know how you told me you'd hold me un - til

- -'ry time I scratch my nails down some - one else -'s back, I hope you

you died, 'til you died? But you're still a - live. And I'm here _____ } to re - mind _

feel it. Well, can you feel it? Well, I'm here _____ }

_____ you _____ of the mess _____ you left _____ when you went a - way. It's not

fair _____ to de - ny _____ me of the cross _____ I bear _____ that you gave

To Coda II

to me. You, _ you, _ you ought - a know. _ You seem ver -

To Coda I

- - y well, things look peace - ful.

I'm not quite _ as well, I thought _ you _ should know. _

Did _ you for - get a - bout me, _ Mis - ter Du - plic - i - ty? I hate to

bug you in the mid - dle of _ din - ner. _ It _ was a slap in the face, how quick - ly

CODA I

D.S. al Coda II

CODA II